I0843425

BOOT ON NECK

by Karen Kellock Ph.D.

Manual for Superior Men

A complete theory based on Einstein physics,
Political Psychology, Systems Theory
and Archetypal Psychiatry.

FORMULA

All success attraction
All disease obstruction
All recovery elimination

You must fast on all three

OBSTRUCTIONS:

People
Habit
Food

BOOT ON NECK

Dys-Eugenics: When every generation is worse than the last and the smart are blocked by lunatics.   Wicked men hypnotize weak women in their houses: trauma results in collapsed boundaries and morals after adapting to the heedless, careless, selfish and callous. At best they become gross social princesses.   They gossip like high school mean girls and we cower fearing they'll do it some more.   The vindictive gossip owns you that way, as a rudder for control--it's witchcraft ok?

THEY DIDN'T CARE

THEY DIDN'T CARE

KAREN KELLOCK CLASS

Karen Kellock Class 1. The obstruction to talents: for success we must manage the narcissists around us.

How interesting that being a "feminist" means becoming more masculine and callous.

He may not be glamorous but he provides fertile soil for her to expand and that's the best man.

Satan makes family members you worst nightmare and it's a tidal wave that'll sweep you up dear.

PTSD is terrible in this era. That's how bad the situations are coming from liberalism in America.

Oh, so she wants you back: Have you forgotten how she kicked you to the curb Jack?

THEY DIDN'T CARE ABOUT YOU

They didn't care what happened to you as a result of what they did. They loved doing it instead.

They had FUN at your expense and even your own family did this! The truth is our friend sis.

Tho' discarded like an old shoe you shot up with the New You in the greatest story ever told too.

People love to feel superior and discard the inferior but they still have to pay the piper for it later.

BOOT
ON
NECK
KAREN KELLOCK

THEY DIDN'T CARE

It's your great energy triggering hatred in them and this is a black hole you must eventually abandon.

I kept feeling it [hatred, they hate me, I'm misjudged & persecuted]: this black cloud must be lifted.

Your great energy triggers fear in them then you're blamed for everythin'. Let this go too hon'.

Only repentance overcame all this. We want crutches when unjustly accused: these are our sins.

PURIFY OR REMAIN VICTIM

Only repentance [making us pure] and understanding crosses the great divide to abundance/no cry.

Purify your image [subliminally understood] and they don't misjudge you anymore, that's the score.

When you relapse back into memory—fighting them, the gossip, the calumny—you work on that see.

Purity thru repentance deals with that black cloud so you can RELEASE it to catapult up right now.

They don't wanna hear that for they love their precious sins. Be a lightning rod anyway friend.

They'd rather blame you then give up sins or live your way. This changes with increased charisma ok.

They'd rather have obscure religiosity then just repent. It's ALL about sins given up, not just for lent.

FALSE RELIGION IGNORES SIN

BLAH BLAH but not a thing about repentance. On and on you go about other things don't you dunce.

THEY DIDN'T CARE

If you've got talent--which you do--you gotta get pure to give them for the Lord and your reward.

He doesn't wanna talk about sin cuz he's a whoremonger on the side. It's legal in Ca, aye.

She doesn't wanna talk about sins cuz she's Mrs. Social Charm with a perfect image/ho harm.

Once the black cloud disperses you go up, and up, and up to a new realm where you're unperturbed.

You've divorced that lower matrix and now when it happens there's an instant rejection sis.

I felt hated and I hated. It was a low matrix and I was addicted as the only way to deal with it.

See it as a problem and focus on it. I think many of us never thought about it but just accepted it.

It is not your job to save someone who continually abandons you at their convenience sis.

ATTENTION WHORES

They maintain their self-perception by the attention of those around them: it's how he's wired ma'am.

Even if things are going right they'll attack for no reason--because they need an adversary son.

When you see these tricks, go grey rock, that's all. This guy is dangerous but you can have a ball.

Women never get over a narcissistic mother who's in competition with her own daughter.

How to deal with husband: end every sentence with "honey" then get away so he can enjoy his day.

THEY DIDN'T CARE

It's hard to believe they are predictable discarders but that's the way they're set up I swear.

Joyce Meyers says it's ok to get tattoos when the bible clearly says we're not to look like fools.

We're not to mark up our bodies like the crazy heathen do. Look it up--you can read it too.

It just doesn't occur to me to eat meat. I'm more likely to choose a succulent salad with cheese.

NEVER RUSH COMPLETION

Don't rush completion and never let anyone push you son. In fact slow it all down/take a vacation.

The narcissist sees his discard as a temporary thing since he owns you and never ends it really.

Feeling unloved, rejected and abandoned puts you in a cocoon that brings on the same events.

They say our major problem is not eating this or that but actually it's eating too much that does it.

From mom's eruption the child feels abandoned, rejected and neglected--it's a feeling in the gut.

Going off to church camp doesn't erase the gut ache, he's incapable of dealing with that too ok.

With my first beer at 15 the black cloud dispersed and I was in hell but it sure felt like heaven at first.

INSTANTLY ADDICTED

When drugs or alcohol take away that black cloud it's an immediate addiction and I know it well.

THEY DIDN'T CARE

It's the bad associations which cater to the gut-ache of rejection so they too become addictions.

Terrfied, lonely and disqualified socially she becomes increasingly isolated and more of an anomaly.

Because of all these challenges you built WISDOM in resistance and are truly a marvel sis.

Feelings of abandonment bring dysfunction and the inability to fit in more until hitting bottom.

Hitting bottom is when you turn it around & don't give a dam cuz it's about you & God not "THEM".

STAY AN INDIVIDUAL NOW

You're an individual now, not enmeshed in a system dumb as cows. It's a giant springboard, wow!

Around sixty people don't care what others think so much: the separation has begun as such.

Hitting bottom [on society & misjudgment] is when one man becomes a majority and is finally over it.

The chosen ones are usually rejected by family and this oughta bring you great relief, surely.

You're an INDIVIDUAL not enmeshed in the family system but you're always cordial to them.

You overcoming them or the narcissist discard makes you a different energy and far higher see.

THEY'RE OFF TO NEW SUPPLY

They're off to new supply and not growing but you became a human dynamo from overcoming.

THEY DIDN'T CARE

He has no object constancy. He loves you now but then forgets, bedazzled by his new supply see.

The main characteristic of narcissism is the sudden DISCARD without closure or even explanation.

There are just as many female narcissists and they treat people--friends or lovers--the same, like sh*t.

Read Mommie Dearest [on Joan Crawford] to see why one never gets over a narcissistic mother.

Where rejection splinters, demons enter. This is when the fake friends & family come in to take over.

THE TRADITIONS OF MEN

The traditions of men & expectations from precedent were the constricting girdles of the moment.

I didn't like any of it and just wanted to be alone to appreciate God in the unique moment.

With trouble, they seek company while I seek solitude. They are pees in a pod and that means rude.

The more you're in the right the more opposition you will face. President Donald J. Trump

Just when overwhelmed by chaos/hostility, your positive emotions shut off: depression/anxiety.

I was hit by false accusation from all sides and everything shut off in a life of a castoff.

Not only suffering with negative emotion but no forward movement, being stuck in that predicament.

They start out in error, lose their frames of reference then bloat out into the chaotic underworld.

THEY DIDN'T CARE

TDS: WHY WOMEN HATE TRUMP

TDS: troubled women cannot distinguish male authority and competence and male tyrannical power.

When the fate & destiny of our republic was in one man: Donald Trump, Geo. Washington, Abe Lincoln.

In America a crisis of legitimacy is happening at breakneck speed: not trusting our country.

The media has become hostile to our country, Christians, conservatives, even the west see.

MISS THEM BUT STAY AWAY

You can miss a person every day and still be grateful they are out of your life. Oprah Winfrey

When your primary thing is to please people you shift from your destiny which is to please God.

A lion can't fit in with cats. But the world deceives us into believing it's superior to multi-adapt.

God didn't make us loners but He doesn't want us to associate with the wrong crowd either.

Friendship with the world is enmity with God. Jesus didn't try to fit in with the Pharisees at all.

The brain starts to minimize after fifty: the only answer is to be more orderly which is best anyway.

Satan will raise people up against the Christian so he'll give up on Christ. It's family members, aye.

They're ok til you start to escape or change then all hell breaks loose and you see the deranged.

THEY DIDN'T CARE

That was all the left brain and it tires me. My work is right brain and it's all completely inspiring.

The only answer to encroaching senility which includes everybody is to become simpler/more orderly.

Signs you were chosen by God, as part of the Elect: you never fit in & the social you may have hated.

As a teen Joseph was a family outcast and his brothers hated him. With the Elect it's common.

REVERTING TO OPPOSITES

The outcast and disowned slave Joe became the most powerful man in Egypt next to Pharaoh

As a triple Pisces with oceanically deep emotions I don't get involved and I stay in my beloved home.

We are in the world but not of it. We cogitate on human relations since they don't understand us.

We are not of this weird world but are meant to change it so we question everything: what a curse.

To deal with people staring in public the Elect gets even more sequestered until leadership.

Every time you deal with a person when intuition said to avoid em it turns out horrible: bedlam.

In the spiritual realm getting involved can strike terrible blows. From me one who knows, don't go.

TRUST YOUR DISCERNMENT

All you gotta do is trust your discernment & save yourself decades of self-disgust if you didn't.

THEY DIDN'T CARE

Your discernment comes from God: a gift so you can move and operate [or separate & relocate].

How many times have you beat yourself up for not listening to your misgivings at the start?

They had fun being corrupt as they told others about you thinking you were down on your luck.

It hurts to face lifelong sister abuse when her image has been so nice, good, helpful and virtuous.

GOD'LL GET EM BACK

God'll get em back, I promise you that. I've seen it all thru life: they don't get away with nothin' Jack.

You came back a shining diamond after they thought you were out for the count or dead man.

Disgusting: They loved hurting you and they set you up for it. The dirtiest you can conger, they did it.

When they went against you--God's anointed--they went against God. The bible says as much.

God's punishments on envious heathen are far beyond anything you could do so just wait Sue.

YOU CAME OUT STRONGER

Your eye had not weakened, you had not grown old. You were beautiful & bold having made gold.

"I've seen jealous detractors lose their spouse, their house and then they went". Lady survivor

Modern women are bold yet for wrong cause but with wholeness energy becomes a power rod.

THEY DIDN'T CARE

You're a thoroughbred--high on the "T" scale--and they can't stand it but sure want to be it.

They spread evil wicked thoughts about you. They incited riots and took you for a fool.

THEY WON'T GET AWAY WITH IT

Sin creates mental illness and like all sinners I had this. You usually can't see it until far later sis.

They will **NOT** get away with this, that's what you gotta know sis. Now be sweet & wash your dishes.

Whenever victimized they were painted in the wrong. It's a terrible thing to be misjudged hon'.

Once we separate we don't hate them. We just cut em out then no more fears of encroachment.

God chose His Elect, that's a biblical fact. Do you really think being His chosen has no effect or lack?

BRAIN MIXUP/MENTAL ILLNESS

Brains are powerful computers so feed em crazy things like AI or DEI and it takes crazy detours.

Would-be genius conforms to narratives or schools of thought but true genius would go crazy or rot.

When you tell a lie you lie to yourself then the brain capacity continually tries to figure it all out.

You lie then project things to cover up the lie. For every sin there's a compensation in the present, aye.

LACTO-FRUITARIAN AND CHOCOLATE

Anorexia is a genetic potential. An event occurs and the symptoms roll out as if to a life schedule.

THEY DIDN'T CARE

Sometimes you gotta expand to contract. I had to go carnivore for awhile but now I am back.

So that's lacto-fruitarian, the best for me. Read my five books from 2001: cheese is adequate protein.

It's not my nature to grill a steak. I'm more into cutting a salad or frying up broccoli with cheese ok.

How about some egg or fish, or shrimp on your salad along with the cheese, that's Greek sis.

But I've gone beyond the starchivore thing, it didn't suffice. I need fat: butter & cheese not rice.

Bread or even tortillas give me trouble. It's gotta be fruit or animal but using dairy for the fat/gold.

It's not in my nature and must be recognized: I prefer cheese and butter for what I need, aye.

I left bacon behind for broccoli and cheese or Greek salad, tho' I'd eat it again if offered, aye.

You gotta expand to constrict. That means to explore all presented avenues only then to reject.

END THOUGHTS

Thru the creative process I've grown so I don't wanna look back down at old projects done.

Government has grown beyond the consent of the governed and that means unelected tyrants.

The sanctimony of the left when they're spewing stupid things is remarkable to me. Mark Levin

It's just social psychology: little things can become a huge dangerous cloud engineered socially.

THEY DIDN'T CARE

Given that kind of traumatic tension the brain would mess up son, especially a genius: no fun.

The SOTU lasted one hour, seven minutes and Joe Biden laid into Trump from start to finish.

Trump secured the border with existing laws so don't give me that blah that you need more pal.

SOCIAL TYRANNY

SOCIAL IS ALL TO THE MOB
THE CRUSHING COLLECTIVE
PUSHED TO BE SOCIAL
LEFT-BRAIN APPROACH TO SOCIAL
BOUNDARIES AND EMOTIONAL COMFORT
WOMEN AND THE HAPPY SPIRIT
HAPPY FROM INSIDE OUT
IN CHARGE OF HER OWN MONEY
CLEARING MIND OF WHAT THEY THINK
YOU WEREN'T WRONG JUST OUTA LINE
FINDING YOUR VOICE
CAVEAT ON FRIENDS
RECAP AND THOUGHTS

SOCIAL TYRANNY

SOCIAL IS ALL TO THE MOB

The world flowed in and I'd become the worst of the lot. I need solitude to be what God wants.

The first lesson of the knight is how fast the world can turn on you. Don't get complacent Sue.

The nonconformist may hear inner voices yelling at em cuz that's all they ever heard as victim.

You're famous and loved today, they all may hate you tomorrow for that is the human condition ok.

It's not so much that I went wrong I was just weak and stupid with no boundaries and flaccid.

We're all filthy sinners: even you, even me. But at least we try while they don't give a dam see.

We are simply an ideological experiment and from the sorry look of things it's not working out.

THE CRUSHING COLLECTIVE

Being made to conform to the collective spirit crushed me. I felt homesick and terrified, unfree.

I hated the groupie spirit invading my home. I felt so alienated and unhappy save being alone.

School Phobia: even in kindergarten I felt like vomiting. I was so unhappy til I returned home see.

The social [loyalty to the group] replaced the individual [personal autonomy] so we were the black sheep

SOCIAL TYRANNY

In the sixth grade we had a weeklong camping retreat and I spent the whole time in the infirmary.

Closed in with those people, without R & R on the side was just too much, I simply wanted to die.

Even talking like this was banned. I was not allowed to speak on how the collective spirit is flawed.

PUSHED TO BE SOCIAL

Even your sister pushing you into being social when you couldn't care less about it all, feeling flawed.

Men could be unique but it's not allowed in female culture and elder sisters are cruel sir.

It's the end result of petty censoring not specific incidents, sickening to any truth-seeker or patriot.

Clash: You were the gypsy spirit--raw, creative, unmoldable--and they were dumbed down and hateful.

The worst thing about prison is CLOSED IN with people with no boundaries or separation at all.

Are you mad at him or mad at yourself for letting him in? Drill down: you were both younger then.

The individual, nothing. The people, everything. For standing up for creativity they hated me?

When confronted with such mediocrity my spirit screeched in silence but I put up with it.

LEFT-BRAIN APPROACH TO SOCIAL

I tried to be social, I red Dale Carnegie. It wasn't me so addictions set in to resist social tyranny.

SOCIAL TYRANNY

When social replaced the individual it all went to hell. I was in the middle, I maladapted to it all.

Anyone not following the green eco mainstream or immigration gets a Nazi classification.

If you can trace all problems to drinking then obviously that's a problem area don't you think?

They hate you for being teachers pet or the best and rave reviews brings their hatred too.

If drinking makes you angry you're probably an alki cuz it's an allergy see, like a demonic spree.

My mother had to wrestle with the demons in me and I the devil in her: those harrowing years.

BOUNDARIES AND EMOTIONAL COMFORT

Too much porous activity erodes UNITY. We must decide the edges of emotional comfort see.

It's highly personal: where are YOU discomforted, what causes distress? It's comparisons I'd guess.

It was a heavenly marriage at first hon' but then the world came in, the hedges down = RUIN.

He was gregarious and porous; I was reclusive, a loner and sick of all this so our unity dispersed.

When he let the world in he simultaneously put me down for my reclusivity, seen as social deviancy.

A HAPPY SPIRIT is the major feminine booster despite the undertow described, the down-putter.

I have a cheerful happy spirit every day and if obstructed in any way you'll be out ok.

SOCIAL TYRANNY

When a woman is "just happy" it emotes a feminine energy irresistible to man, world, family.

A superior female won't hang in, fighting to be an option. She will bow out and go on vacation.

I'm either number ONE [no other options or comparisons] or I'm gone: that's a queen son.

Stop living in delusion. You want this guy [that's all you know hon'] but he's not responding or is gone.

WOMEN AND THE HAPPY SPIRIT

We don't see "happy spirit" when stress forces her outside her essence, carrying two loads in a sense.

Her Creator didn't intend a full-time job so what's impacted first is countenance [madness].

Her countenance plays a massive role in her feminine presentation: you gotta be happy woman.

See a woman with a stern countenance and we assume she's difficult, an old crone, a neurotic adult.

The world assumes she's masculine and angry when the reality is she's burdened/overworked ok.

HAPPY FROM INSIDE OUT

True queens learn sooner or later that happiness is produced not procured and it's all INNER.

But if you start ragging on me or triangulating with others it's a downputter and joy killer.

A woman can't go without and buy it, she must produce it from within--that's her accomplishment.

SOCIAL TYRANNY

If dependent on outer for happiness then join herself to another and she's even more obstinate.

She's happy from inside out: that's being firmly formed when happiness is authentic and consistent.

A happy woman feels at peace--she feels SAFE. She feels provided for/valued by herself ok.

A happy woman must like her reflection in the mirror. Not for him or them but herself for sure.

When her clothes fit right without bumps and bulges her self-esteem shoots thru the roof, honest.

She knows how exercise improves the mental, how it changes her perspective too you know.

IN CHARGE OF HER OWN MONEY

She's great when in charge of her own money. Then she can rest in her feminine and just be happy.

Low quality gals look to guys for money, queens go and get it for themselves so they're happy.

Now she will approve of men with the money philosophy that is consistent with her own see.

She's the biblical female with her own. When merged with a man's own it's bingo, the royal couple.

To the hippies: A feast is for laughter and wine maketh merry but money answers ALL THINGS.

It takes financial resources so problems aren't an issue and they're easily fixed in a minute too.

If there's money there's less stress and drama with far more stability and a happy momma.

SOCIAL TYRANNY

A queen conscious woman takes charge of the money because that keeps the home happy.

A queen will attract a rich cat, never settling on a man content having nothing/never building.

How can a queen conscious woman be happy broke? A clown in a crown, lascivious loser she joked.

A woman gotta know everything's all right, we got things covered. Not month to month, flustered.

Now that she knows it's all covered she can sit back and enjoy the movie, directing the show see.

No one guarantees a providing husband. She must provide for herself/have a future sense.

To rest in her highest frequency she must know inside provision's not an issue then get busy.

For her to be happy money can't be an issue. He gotta bring the money if he wants the honey Sue.

A woman can't be happy when overly concerned about provisions and happy wives raise incomes.

CLEARING MIND OF WHAT THEY THINK

Shut it down while the ball's still in your court. When you sense a shift cut it loose/go forward.

Indoctrination is the seed of sadness and anxiety in a woman. You must clear your mind hon'.

Most women are so full of people's opinions they're a haunted house/don't make good friends.

If full of what others think of her she's emotionally highjacked without ever realizing it sir.

SOCIAL TYRANNY

YOU WEREN'T WRONG JUST OUTA LINE

You didn't do anything that crazy or horrible you just went against the grain that's all.

There's just something about you which is so ineffably different and they aim to get you for it.

By being alive you went against the grain your whole life: walking out of synchrony it was strife.

I knew something would happen to change our direction cuz divine discontent always brings it on.

A most important mission for any woman: to become impervious save fans & fame, a new game

The undertow is so severe [so maligned for years] she achieves success exhausted but pure.

She'd rather give it away than have you get it. That's like in high school, fake friendships.

Be a weirdo all the way to the bank, or mal-adapt to the dark and dank dungeon of what they think.

When flustered always recall and see: they don't own reality, you do and they're all crazy.

FINDING YOUR VOICE

I wasn't always this way, I was severely silenced by society and was muted for decades.

But the truth couched in verse is less suspect and mysteriously gets past censure I guess.

In drawing lines and boundaries to evil children I came off as a harridan and it was bedlam.

SOCIAL TYRANNY

Just say to him/her: I'm not happy when you come. Let them figure out why you reject the bum.

Look forward to retirement. You're still working at what you love but free of structure like prison.

Pure, your true [predesigned] spirit's in you and you can proceed with continuous revelation too.

Now you're free, above the crowd/madness all around. Now, finally, every moment's your own.

CAVEAT ON FRIENDS

They're insincere, invasive and treacherous. They're not your friends just users of the virtuous.

You're alone at the end but then you bust thru to new life, surrounded by good and true friends.

All you put up with on the lower rungs, yuk! But how else to learn it [didn't get it from mom].

I had to see the truth about people to be a true Christian with lines and boundaries against sin.

People betray you, they come and go but God is eternal and is always there: on high, so below.

People are creepy, they blame you for what THEY do. It's frustrating as "hell" when Satan rules.

Love God first, that's the point. Then love people all you want but don't forget, they disappoint.

I don't mind waiting cuz I always see imperfections needing mending or areas for clearing.

I don't mind waiting cuz I've learned to be content in a tiny dusty cabin or a big homestead mansion.

SOCIAL TYRANNY

I don't mind waiting cuz I've already been rewarded anyway as God provides and sanctifies.

God blessed me before the work was even done so earthly rewards don't concern me none.

What do I care for fame, it's just another invasion of the private domain but it is confirming ok.

Fame is necessary to water the crop/catch the fish and that's how I'll see it not be thrilled by it.

RECAP AND THOUGHTS

Kanye: I'm not saying he doesn't have a right to say it, just that he's a pissant for saying it.

The Great Replacement is when the dominant group is replaced by a minority, and it's treachery.

I write, study and think--that's my whole life from A-Z. I wait for that divine pearl then record it see.

Your work is done, you're waiting to be discovered. It's so exciting cuz you know/are prepared.

BOOT ON NECK

GOSSIP IS A RUDDER OF CONTROL
SURROUNDED BY STRANGERS IS TORTURE
THE COSTS OF BELIEVING A LIE
THE HERO'S PATH IS UP AND DOWN
NO MORE DAM R.V. HOOKUPS
YOU PRIMED EM AGAINST ME
SOCIAL PROMISCUITY VS. YOU'RE THE ONE
DON'T BE THEIR ENTERTAINMENT
THEY THINK THEY OWN YOU
ADDICTION MAINTAINS ITSELF
HUMAN CONTROL THRU GOSSIP
WIFE OF THE ALCOHOLIC SYNDROME
IF YOU SAY YOU'RE WELL YOU'RE SICK
TRAUMA COLLAPSES BOUNDARIES
SENSING TREACHERY IS A GIFT
THEY LACK EMPATHY
THEY FEED ON OUR FEAR
SOUR REACTIONS TO FEMALE THINKERS
CONTROLLED BY SCARCITY FEARS
IT'S THE ARCHETYPES NOT PEOPLE

BOOT ON NECK

FLIP-FLOPS AND SHIT-SHOTS
VICTIM LOSES SELF-FOCUS
DISRUPTIONS AND DISAPPOINTMENTS
SILENT ESCAPE PLANS
HOOKING HER SOUL THRU LANGUAGE
WICKED MEN HYPNOTIZING WEAK WOMEN
NOW SHE'S LOST HER VOICE
TRUMP HATE IS MENTAL ILLNESS
THE NASTY CONDONE PEDERASTY
DINASAUR MEDIA
DEMENTED HOLLYWOOD SCUM
"WHERE'S THE BIGOT" IS SO STUPID
MEN WANT TRANQUILITY, WOMEN SECURITY
FICKLE FEMINISTS
TRUMP IS OPPOSITE TO INSULTS
ZOMBIES CAN'T THINK, EMOTE BY ROTE
HORRIBLE RINOS BUT DEMS ARE TRA
RAISE MORALE, *THEN* RENEWAL
TRUMP NOT A STATUS CLIMBER
SIN: A MAL-ADAPTIVE COPING DEVICE

BOOT ON NECK

SAME DEAD CORNY SCRIPT
PATRIOTS SAVE US FROM GOVERNMENT
OLDER WOMEN SHOULD INSTILL MORALS
LIBERAL CHRISTIANS ARE OXYMORONS
UN-LIBERAL MIDDLE AMERICA
DISFRIEND LIBERALS TO TEACH THE ABLES
PUBLIC SCHOOLS ARE TOXIC
FEMINIST "RAPE CULTURE" BUT ISLAM? UNCONCERNED
HAPPY COMMUNISM IS ILLUSION
ANTIFA THE ENEMY OF AMERICAN CITIZENS
CONFUSED DAYCARE MILLENNIALS
LIBERALISM VS. WISDOM
AMERICAN TRAGEDY: MILLIONAIRES COMPLAINING
RIGHT-WINGERS AND BITTER CLINGERS
FEMINISTS HATE MEN
UNIVERSITIES FURNISH ILLEGAL TRUANTS
JAIL RABBLE LIKE BOW-WOW AND UNCLE
LIBERALS CAN'T ACCEPT DEFEAT
CHURCH OMITS SIN—THE MAIN THING
HOMESTEAD UPDATES

BOOT ON NECK

GOSSIP IS A RUDDER OF CONTROL

"Forgive them Father for they know not what they do". Is there anything more absolutely true?

SICK SYSTEMS: "He was a dam drunk before I even met him but then again I chose to marry him".

Dys-Eugenics: When every generation is worse than the last and the smart are blocked by lunatics.

She gossips like a high school mean girl and you cower before her fearing she'll do it some more.

The vindictive gossip owns you that way. She uses it as a rudder for control—it's witchcraft ok?

The stressed out woman ages quickly so now she's REALLY targeted by hubby and everybody.

Being stressed she makes major mistakes unable to discern good from bad in a moral collapse.

SURROUNDED BY STRANGERS IS TORTURE

There's two signs of God's wrath: natural disasters ad suddenly being surrounded by strangers.

Your very existence attacks their reality--not just their views but their utopian cosmology.

They don't question bringing friends to your house, it's their cosmology: we are one, see?

There are grown boys and grown men. With a boy you better watch yourself or you're dead.

BOOT ON NECK

When kid brings his friends to your house unannounced it's the same dam thing: INVASION

The sick family is like a four-act play which repeats itself daily with only slight variations, so pray.

THE COSTS OF BELIEVING A LIE

Believing a lie ages you. It takes a toll holding it all together despite contradictions in y'all.

Believing a lie causes constant stress & seared vision trying to make sense of insanity all around.

Liberals hate conservatives and you can feel it in your family. It's a vicious break, unfortunately.

They just have a vision--cosmology--which is self-evident/a tautology but is false you see.

Obama putting apartments in single family districts is equalizing things he thinks but it stinks.

Strangers: I see no difference between apartments and Bed & Breakfasts in country neighborhoods.

You got involved with low lifes, that's what you did. Now just admit it, they were losers/twits.

THE HERO'S PATH IS UP AND DOWN

He was a Christian but we all have a tiger inside to tame to do that huge job for which we came.

He was Christian but still lurched at women and lacked self-control in other "hot" situations.

She was Christian but still had appetites she had to curb to focus energy to be the best ever.

BOOT ON NECK

He was Christian but still had to learn to LOOK AWAY rather than stare at women in public ok.

These people are as cruel as they can possibly be but wearing that image you like em see?

I don't wanna adapt to a man in my house. Stop dumping your BF here while you go out.

You think I'm so useless I'm just a waiting station for your friends? I wanna work/get out man.

NO MORE DAM R.V. HOOKUPS

The social generation since WWII has blinded people to the ill effects of their bad associations.

I give you an opportunity for solitude in nature and you brought all your friends to my ruin, major.

Stop using me as a pit stop. I'm busy and don't need your company but you surely need me.

No you can't use me as your RV hookup. Yah we got lotsa land but want privacy from screwups.

No you can't park your RV on my land cuz last time you brought your friends/lovers/brothers man.

Don't come around to charge your phone or use the John. Hook up your RV then be gone.

Last time you took over my home. That's when I thought I needed you with boundaries low.

YOU PRIMED EM AGAINST ME

All sick systems are self-isolating as flying monkeys hate you--her other friend--automatically.

BOOT ON NECK

No you can't park your people in my home while you roam around stop using me man.

I see your friends & family hate me--why is that Jezebel? They've obviously primed by you gal.

You imposed on me constantly & your friends bugged me. The whole thing was an imposition see?

It woulda been fine but then you brought all those other people into it. Why so insecure you idiot?

My home is not your phone charger. You gotta go to town for that/you're becoming a bummer.

SOCIAL PROMISCUITY VS. YOU'RE THE ONE

You like me but then a thousand other people like we're on the same level. What an insult devil.

There is a conspiracy against privacy. They see it as a hideous thing, your isolation from lunacy.

You didn't come to see me but to borrow things apparently or bring evil tidings/gossiping.

Be SICK of the inferior relationships you've had and start a new life now, a superior chap.

I don't like your dependency. How dare you--take your clothes down to the laundromat sonny.

I fear violence cuz you being immature see my boundaries as rejection and want revenge I fear.

Drop every deadhead in your life and attract NOW a mass of high life levels without this strife.

They worm their way in then take over your home. You see you're still a woman and them a man.

He comes in and yells it's too hot or cold. He's mad it isn't what he likes--this is disrespect girl.

Reject beauty-hating philistines: uncultured, indecent, gross, imposing and socially hypnotized.

They're angry speech fascists so of course you're afraid to go there and talk about this or that.

He always came around when I was fixing lunch. Or dinner--any time he wanted pleasure.

He wanted to get in cuz he loved what I do. I make things nice & have it all in the pad too.

DON'T BE THEIR ENTERTAINMENT

They will use you for their entertainment. They're bored and lonely and you're the creative man.

They wanna get you outa the house when you just wanna stay home. No more discussion.

They **PRESSURE** you to get outa you house. They wanna get you out and away far off.

They come on your turf changing all your plans. No man, you come here we do what I am.

They worm their way in then later their friends arrive. It's a set up, an army coming for strife.

Take a long people fast then start a **FORMAL** lifestyle: no unannounced drop-ins pal.

They arrive unexpectedly then rag on you about not being more accessible to their treachery.

They demand you go to their boring useless meetings of ego gatherings and social manipulations.

BOOT ON NECK

The groupies & joiners have no inner life cuz if they did this meetingitis thing they'd rise above.

THEY THINK THEY OWN YOU

They think they own you. They act like it too, shaming you for being so dam private/busy too.

I know it's near impossible to find a decent friend but don't settle for less until then or its death.

The dominant one controls gossip flow and that's the human race which is socialized you know.

Arguing with a liberal is like hitting your head with a hammer--feels good when you stop.

I'll admit it was a soul tie at first but when I learned about narcissists I overcame the sadist.

They're not gonna talk about sin/repentance of hell/heaven if their pastor is a lesbian.

Biden's like an arsonist setting fire to a house then blaming the firefighters for the chaos.

Plato's best advice: Learn about your politics or inferior men will rule over you and even despise.

ADDICTION MAINTAINS ITSELF

There doesn't have to be a reason for the addiction for the addictive process maintains itself.

It's the replacement of legacy Americans with more obedient cultures from far-away countries.

They're not gonna talk about sin/repentance OR hell/heaven if their pastor is a lesbian.

Black female mayors defunding the police but then beefing up personal protection, please.

Anyone not fitting a particular everchanging narrative is being banned--it's getting scary in America.

I prefer to let it develop organically--on it's own, as it will--then preplan and see it fall down.

HUMAN CONTROL THRU GOSSIP

Land is more important than silver or gold. LAND is a buffer zone/earth you can call your own.

Tyranny is the norm in the world, liberty's been the exception. Now tyranny's back again.

Calumny is soul murder: destroying your reputation. The gossip is hell on earth, feminism.

The gossip gets POWER that way and doesn't care who pays. The sheriff's her best friend, ok?

It was hardly a resort town or place to relax. It was a prison of gossip and Lord, I hated that!

In cowboy country we live our own life. We're ingrown, it's about the household/no more strife.

How I suffered--how I watched others suffer--with the gossip which feminists use as a rudder.

The men were different save a male homosexual who officiously ruined reputations in like ways.

In a small town gossip's not just a rudder but a tsunami maker: relocate or be ruined forever.

WIFE OF THE ALCOHOLIC SYNDROME

BOOT ON NECK

He always. comes to me when things go dark but once pumped up he goes away of course.

Her alcoholic was a jolly social manipulator so as it is with the poor wife everyone blamed her.

No one knew of the pure emotional torture going on in the home and she's blamed for all wrongs.

Being blamed for his actions causes so much frustration she starts drinking to her own destruction.

Due to his drunken insults her appearance fades or distorts and now she's more of a target.

IF YOU SAY YOU'RE WELL YOU'RE SICK

As the whole system comes down on her she locks herself in the smallest room in fear.

These were her family and friends so their sudden turn brings fear--the panic of betrayal dear.

Few see the system dynamics when in it so they decompensate agreeing they're the lunatic.

The only way to make em nice to her is to agree she's the one who is mentally disordered.

If she stands up for herself contending he's the drunkard she's called sick again/the target.

Agree you're sick, get smiling congratulations. Contend you're well, you're back in the institution.

If she dares complain about her alki husband she's called mean bitch in her false accusations.

By the time he gets sober and all this is swept under the rug she really collapses in decompensation.

BOOT ON NECK

TRAUMA COLLAPSES BOUNDARIES

Trauma results in collapsed boundaries and morals. Almost unaware It's a vicious thing for girls.

Without a home, personal boundaries or morals she falls into a pit becoming whatever AFFECTS her.

Owning my own home with a fence and locked gate in a safe place was my biggest achievement ok.

But now I understand why I couldn't' stand my peers and each generation gets worse for sure.

These people are heedless, careless, selfish, callous, a dirty dish mess, gross social princesses.

They will do anything they can to you, anything they can get away with. Do not trust one my dearest.

For we're in an entirely new world. See Seattle, San Diego worse than a third world slum. Come Lord!

SENSING TREACHERY IS A GIFT

After surviving my wars I can sense treachery in an instant and that is the mark of a true leader I guess.

The signs of disrespect are everywhere and no one knows what to do so gotta train em to respect you.

Without morals or God a human becomes a mere cartoon caricature and in some cases subhuman.

All of a sudden Germans started picking on their Jewish neighbors, attacking them even, squealing.

The rich man is a popular man but go bankrupt now see how many friends you have, that's the test.

BOOT ON NECK

What you see is emotional immaturity. Very few are mature even in old age and signs are clear.

Without morals it's a rudderless ship hitting to and fro while godlessly banking on who you know.

Without morals creativity stops, you are empty and it shows--you're a flop so now call on God.

As the ego crashes and burns, humility [from humiliation] is your saving grace making you the ACE.

THEY LACK EMPATHY

Normals are curbed from violence by imagining how that would feel but narcissists have no empathy.

Since they have no empathy their violent response crosses that line thus you FEAR them.

Don't cross a narcissist lest you haven't learned your lesson yet cuz his paybacks are sadistic.

You see the problem, bide your time, NEVER confide, pray for a way out and when it comes you RUN/HIDE.

You can never fight with a narcissist and expect to get anywhere. Silently, be led out by God sister.

He wants you scared cuz that's his feed for the day. He'll sadistically drop you off in other cities.

I became a sweet yes person to the narcissist while waiting for a way out. Be wise--no insults.

All he wants is adulation so by being a chameleon for awhile is just good thinkin' before escapin'.

Don't think I'm gonna let em in here with the possibility of turning on me suddenly, including flying monkeys.

BOOT ON NECK

You fight with him or call him an old codger then get ready for vengeance beyond slaughter.

You dumbly burnt your bridges and moved in with him and now you're trapped in his sadistic lion's den.

Narcissists: I could see he was feeding on my fear. Since I feared for my pets they were his targets.

THEY FEED ON OUR FEAR

I was hypersensitive so he fed on my extreme reactions. There was never a time for true relaxation.

He sweetly invited me to live on his fancy Arabian horse ranch before I walked into his sadistic crunch.

Don't put yourself at anyone's mercy, do not trust things will work out, let go of foolish fantasies.

Women want love so bad they see what they wanna see until it's too late and they seek only escaping.

Because we have a compelling emotional response [empathy] it curbs our behavior to enemies.

Never fear losing people cuz they're just archetypes who come and go as lessons from our lows.

Wow, the shock of seeing their true self come out suddenly when at first they'd acted so sweetly.

If you're rich, popular or have something they need they'll be nice for awhile despite the tiger inside.

Don't forget, it's always good at first. He's charismatic and exciting but soon you'll feel cursed.

The narcissist is ultimately boring cuz he's empty inside. Tho' an actor, soon revealed is his other side.

BOOT ON NECK

Tho' it's sad when he collapses under the weight of image-magic you can't help it so step back.

The narcissist is so dangerous in his likely vengeance going way beyond what is normal justice.

SOUR REACTIONS TO FEMALE THINKERS

If you're a female thinker your life is near torture cuz they react to you as danger cuz you don't cower.

No matter what he does he can't get it back and same with the female narcissist--she widens/dims.

She'll start fighting with her husband tho' it was he who gave her the confidence/strength to do so.

When you see your handsome/pretty mentors take on a moon face suddenly or go dim in any way.

Yes it happens to all of us this vacillation BUT the champions learn to constrain the variant.

Don't fantasize about how he's gonna turn out great like you want--it's all from early trauma mate.

Having been rejected as an infant of course you seek to fill that slot, correct the wrong, be held all night.

This is why love addiction's the most obdurate one: the prevalence of early trauma from feminism.

We weren't way out there to cater to her. We had our own life for which we cut all ties and then matured.

Don't fantasize about how he's gonna turn out great like you want--it's all from early trauma mate.

The worst narcissists are kids. They have no lines nor boundaries and now it's legal to trespass.

BOOT ON NECK

Many renowned stars may've had a checkered past, it comes from being curious and passionate.

But they had to resolve those problems and repent in order to realize their destiny/no more hid.

Even if someone's hurt us there's a line the healthy don't cross but that the narcissist will always.

CONTROLLED BY SCARCITY FEARS

The narcissist uses intimidation/scarcity: Keep talking and I'm gonna leave you/put you in poverty.

It scarcity or fear you're going to lose something which is the key to you being controlled by him.

He's worked hard and your brain is now psychologically and chemically addicted to the abuse cycle.

Energy sugar breakfast: sweet fruit smoothie, cliff bar, grape juice, sugar gummy bears and dates.

I need the sugar for glucose energy and that is more important to me than other food matrices.

I am getting more into Fuhrman's micronutrients: cut up veggies dipped in yogurt green goddess.

The majority of Republicans are wimps and cowards but there's a new wave who will stand up and fight.

They stand behind armored cars and velvet ropes and have no idea what we go thru us dopes.

He has so much trouble facing himself he insists: can't we stay positive? Then he gets on with it.

What caused ALL the trouble? OTHER PEOPLE. Had I been left to myself I coulda avoided evil.

BOOT ON NECK

His Philistine family looked down on him constantly and spread vicious gossip around town/country.

Fanaticism is the only form of will power to which the weak and irresolute can rise. Nietzsche

It's impossible to have normal brain function/healthy emotions when eating mostly fast food. Fuhrman

Don't fret those people. People vary but the archetypes and system dynamics are the same: evil.

Don't put your cards on the table, leave silently. For if he knows he'll get the upper hand honey.

IT'S THE ARCHETYPES NOT PEOPLE

Forget the specific people, these were just archetypes evoked by your bad behavior for sure.

With a narcissist it has nothing to do with who **YOU** are as a person but what you can do for **THEM**.

To demand equal time [a little time for you] gets you put on the narcissist's shit list and very quick.

Time for you deems you **USELESS** to the narcissist as your replacement is quickly slid into place.

Never give ultimatums. If he thinks you're fed up and about to leave he'll discard and be mean.

I was scared of what he'd do next so became sweeter not bitchier planning my escape outa there.

You don't fight a psychopath you become more compliant. Think escape, he can't control your mind.

I was so sweetly complaint he figured he had me in the bag then I escaped after making contacts.

BOOT ON NECK

You can't advise the narcissist cuz who are you to advise him? Any suggestions are presumptuous sin.

FLIP-FLOPS AND SHIT-SHOTS

He was so sweet at first and I had such a love thirst I put myself at his mercy and then he TURNED...

Stop "falling" for people and distrust all such siren calls. Question your attractions until you are well.

How come you changed so much in a year? Was it wrong diet, wrong actions or precisely what dear?

So I lived in a shack way out in the boondocks just to escape the liberal herd of losers and cucks.

Churches acted like I didn't have the right to be so happy way out there--I was to be social dear.

They took it as insult I didn't wanna socialize with them but'd rather stay in my happy lonely cabin.

They had to discount me in some way to make their own social trip legit and call it a Christian church.

Mr. and Mrs. Social Charm get chosen for deacons, isn't that exactly my point--the church has fallen.

VICTIM LOSES SELF-FOCUS

Codependent manages emotions of the narcissist rather than realize what she's losing in the matrix.

Antisocial personality disorder: morality/legality means nothing they just pushback society's norms.

They move animalistically: whatever their goal prompts them to do there are no restrictions too.

BOOT ON NECK

They have no remorses and if you're in a dispute get ready for great difficulty or he stays aloof.

Often adult psychopaths are stuck in adolescence with Oppositional Defiant Disorder: MESSERS.

They will throw a wrench into all your plans, it's constant opposition tho' subtle until disaster's end.

They hate any and all instruction since it assumes one has domination and this means hell for the moms.

It's a deeply held incorrigible pattern combined with NO conscience about what they do to anything.

DISRUPTIONS AND DISAPPOINTMENTS

With him around you can count on disruptions and disappointments cuz that's what defines him.

On the. contrary I felt vary grateful having that experience of a solitary desert cabin in the wilderness.

But it's something I'd never do today knowing what I now know: a fence/locked gate is the way to go.

Marriage was the prize, it saved me from all this: being overwhelmed by the herd of flying monkeys.

They are so gross, cruel, callous and maladapted you can't help em/help yourself by escaping em.

They were high school '85 and I don't know what they taught em but I was completely terrified.

God help me, these people will do anything and they have NO empathy but they're just children you see.

I can't stand being around that callous immoral generation and just wanna stay alone son, let it be known.

BOOT ON NECK

For even in wartime people still had style, grace and class but not these modern people: crass asses.

This is how you handle remorse: We all have a past and all have skeletons in the closet, get over it.

This is how you handle embarrassment: we've all done it [faux paus] but most if not all are hiding it.

Shame: Yes but you're STILL the best. Think of that not this input from your family or friends.

Remember, no ultimatums/open revenge for they'll get you back 10X worse than you ever planned.

SILENT ESCAPE PLANS

Once the slaveowner senses escape it's THEN he puts the shackles on. Stay compliant and nice hon.

Forget individual players or you'll get hung up. It's the archetypes played out, people are irrelevant.

Lady said "after he sprayed me with a power washer I always said 'honey' and then all went well."

You apparently think I can get over PTSD just by wanting to but these events are in my face like new.

Attracted to earthly things and now you see the sex ain't all that/the money ain't there: you're trapped.

It's good to have a man who's cute but it's much better to have one who's safe with a nurturing spirit.

Life is hard enough but to invite people in who drain you, make you feel foolish, leak your confidences.

Be careful with men. A woman is emotionally built to be sensitive to the opinions of men she esteems.

BOOT ON NECK

And thus if a man she esteems disparages her she struggles with that verbal assault forever.

Problem now: There's a generation of men who literally hates women seeking to break them down.

If you're going for his swag you're opening your heart to emotional abuse: dial it back and pull back in.

The emotional abuse he'll put you through will be more than you ever experienced in your life, aye.

One of the ways the man infuses a soul tie to a woman is by using abusive language--he demeans her.

HOOKING HER SOUL THRU LANGUAGE

His language puts a hook in her soul that she can't seem to shake--the man knows the power of hate.

When the holy spirit says "that's some good rappin' but there's **NO CONTENT**", do not ignore that.

You gotta check for a man's energy. If you don't feel safe, secure, at rest--shut it down/not meant to be.

The hobosexual is immoral. He creeps into the life of a woman and leads her astray with her soul.

The hobo-sexual is immoral but that's what gets her flesh moving. It's a system and she even loves him.

She's turned on by his condescension: insults targeted to humiliate and demean but run the sick system.

A dangerous man manages the soul of a woman with condescension and running her emotions ragged.

He knows he. can manage her emotions by speaking down to her, coming off as superior/smarter.

BOOT ON NECK

He first woos with words making her feel good about self and once hooked he tears her down to hell.

No matter how much less he is in education etc. she will be put in the inferior position and it's locked in.

He takes a brilliant woman and convinces her she's helpless, a total mess without his highness.

Once he had me in that needy position he continued to beat me down to female slave conditioning.

A woman WANTS to look up to a man to feel secure so easily assumes the deprecated position.

WICKED MEN HYPNOTIZING WEAK WOMEN

Wicked men hypnotizing weak women in their houses: He has nothing, she gladly gives him all that's hers.

Think of it: An inferior man can now manage your life cuz he's got a hook in your soul by calling you old.

He had a hook in my soul by reminding me of the original trauma of being rejected by an old crone.

A soothing tongue speaking words that build up and encourage is a tree of life. Prov. 15: 4

But a perverse tongue that overwhelms and depresses crushes the spirit--I can still remember it.

We are talking about a woman with everything inside in love with a man with NOTHING going on, aye?

After all that the first tiny sign of disrespect triggers the hair on her neck and she's gone, that's it.

Literal Ph.D. women are manipulated by uneducated men but even the Ph.D. men are liberal femmes.

BOOT ON NECK

When you called me a yapper that's a small irritating dog. Quite an insult coming from a big male hog.

A woman with something going on managed and manipulated by a man with nothing going on.

And he does this thru language: he's an emotional abuser--abusive but passive aggressive.

Passive-aggressive: No outright insults but facial expressions making you look stupid that's all.

He gets you to a point where you second guess yourself and become so self-conscious you fail.

Now that you nervously don't share anything you're thinking he easily takes over completely.

NOW SHE'S LOST HER VOICE

He's now taken your voice from you and there's no Ph.D. not even a whole human in your shoes.

These narcissists invading you have NO empathy and they have NO compassion, remember that darlin'

HOBO-sexual searches for/exploits the woman's weak points: "laden with sins and lusts". 2 Tim: 3

"Silly women laden with sins and lusts": the hobo-sexual locates where these are and sucks up.

The gist: The hobo-sexual locates her vulnerabilities and controls her through her neediness.

These people search out our weaknesses then wait for the right moment to pounce and devour us.

Managing her life thru her neediness: the biggest is the need to be wanted so flattery is the tactic.

BOOT ON NECK

He's slick with flattery. If you need to be wanted all he needs to do is tell you you're the best of all see.

If you want to be loved so bad then senseless buffoonery gets your blood going and heart fluttering.

Kids are crazy with all their genders. They don't know a thing about politics but are communist defenders.

"Your kids belong to us and we're getting rid of the family". The family breaks down in this engineered reality.

If you go along with this crap (e.g. gender) you'll lose the map of essentials for happiness: old ways are best.

Cops blocked by liberal mayors/can't deport killers: Libs don't care about you and that's why we're bitter.

Their weapons are of no avail. Over goodness and God's will evil will not prevail.

TRUMP HATE IS MENTAL ILLNESS

The deluge of Trump-hate demonstrates the degree of mental illness in states.

Russophobic insanity has taken over.

The left was looking forward to a Hillary Clinton presidency to finish America off for good: that was trendy.

Kids that didn't get what they wanted for birthday so get violent about it: that's the left (and they don't quit).

Alinsky: Accuse others of what you are doing. Dems have been in bed with Russia for 50 years and Hillary's selling.

The backbone/decent people of America must stand up against the bitter people of the entertainment industry.

Demoralize the population cuz when they don't have morals you can bend them as you please.

BOOT ON NECK

Left: Left-hand path, Luciferianism, Satanism, devil worshippers.

The Satanists are in huge rallies against Trump who has invoked God.

Fake media: deceptive, hateful enemy of the people. Globalist, evil.

The media is connected to the ruling class, the deep state, Soros and that's why you can't believe em, sorry.

They get off on you not having something.

Beck's paid/protected like Hillary and Obama. They don't get into trouble but Trump'll end their bubble.

You're bad cuz you freaked out at a man in the bathroom. They sexualize kids by removing gender (doom).

How dare your daughter not wanna see a man's genitals. They're priming for pedophilia and it's getting old.

THE NASTY CONDONE PEDERASTY

I don't care Milo what you say, you said pederasty was all-ok.

Our man's at the Whitehouse working not at frivolous events smirking.

We'll do as we wilt. Witches Law on Trump-haters

Milo the reprobate debauched fallen soul: sudden fall, that's all.

Fire Bill Maher and ban him from TV. He said a boy age 14 raped by female teacher age 35 was all-ok.

They call him "Hitler" though Hitler killed millions and Trump just regulations.

Men respond to the attraction factors of women but are repelled if distasteful/non-nurturing (mother).

Lame media: Stop reporting on how you feel bad cuz no one cares.

We are in a new McCarthyism more frightening than ever before. Lionel

BOOT ON NECK

Demonize them, marginalize them, polarize them, spread hatred and tell lies about the opposition: Alinsky/Lenin.

Liberals, universities, media, professional protestors and Hollywood are all against him: stand against them.

Synagogues of Satan: faith communities, interfaith dialogue, Chrislam, Unity-- Christianity is exclusivity.

Obama was about "cut outs" from laws (exemptions for buddies) but Trump is the rule of law in reality.

Everything Trump has done is existing law.

The first attack against Donald Trump was fired only a few minutes into the Oscars then they kept on coming.

DINASAUR MEDIA

Stick a fork in the dinosaur mainstream media: they're done. Alex Jones

Washington Post, Newsweek, Time call for insurrection/murder of the president--of course he's blocking em.

Anti-God, anti-family: at the bottom of the left is occultism/sex abuse and it easily turns violent too.

We're done with the Oscars, Hollywood and public schools. We're the new inventors and now we're cool.

New religion is political correctness, globalism and break up families and nations--bunch of blobs with no elation.

The best thing about Trump is he's not out to get us. Alex Jones

God hates cowards, abusers of innocence or those weaker than them. That's scripture so be a leader, friend.

The most disenfranchised people under globalism are the ones saying "kill Trump": it's really amazing stuff.

BOOT ON NECK

Get em stultified on social issues that are never rectified while meanwhile they're gang-raped with lies.

The most hated are Glenn Beck and Megyn Kelly. There's just something about a turncoat that's smelly.

Whoopie and sycophants reading off a script then selling their tyranny and lies: that's Hollywood scum you guys.

Actors pushing leftist crap and they don't even believe it. Doing what they're told or insane mentals getting old.

The Oscar anti-Trump fiasco with each star seeing who could get in the biggest jab at our commander-in-chief.

They're not just declaring war on Trump but everyone who voted for him.

Arrogance: "Our goal in politics is the same as our goal in art, and that's to get to the truth." Warren Beatty

DEMENTED HOLLYWOOD SCUM

How could demented Hollywood applaud Iran who kills gays/beheads jews?

Hollywood never thinks of the victims of Iran--they just love it, man.

The drug-addicted perverts can't see the hypocrisy of their stupidity.

Mummies with no ratings, narcissistic sellout scumbags: they're done.

Leftists are not morons they're evil anti-American, anti-individual liberty, pro-collective controlling globalists.

If liberals were morons they couldn't make a dent like this, proving the wrong premise overrides intelligence.

Projecting adulthood on babies is criminal, and treating adults as babies is terrible, the worst of all.

He talks like someone who doesn't understand it (BS) but wants to sound like someone who does.

BOOT ON NECK

Always talking about joy and happiness sounds like a liberal because that's the spiel but it's unreal.

Facing the ugly truth is our only defense. Living in la la land leaves you unprotected: need gate/fence.

Afro-centered or women's studies just teach lies with no accountability so they hate white society.

Arrogant professors, like we're supposed to take on their jargon when it's all so contrived/far out.

Loving liberal females are now often slipping into pugnacity: duking it out with other loving ladies.

They think there's only one prism to see the world: social justice--all is homophobic, racist or sexist.

In everything they do they're searching for a bigot. Two warring parties: which one (can you dig it)?

"WHERE'S THE BIGOT" IS SO STUPID

"Where's the bigot" is so fatuous, stupid, reductionist and depressing. Milo

Socialist deep need for equality, lack of competition and unconditional love transferred to state (GOV).

"Safe" spaces break down barriers between words and action--like there's something trying to hurt them.

Lower IQs cling to repetition to gain security--they don't know what's going on, it's virtual reality.

Poorly educated shallow thinkers cling to slogans and superficial sayings and thoughts: stinkers.

Family breakup due to feminism, media male-bashing and courts. It's eugenics/globalism of course.

BOOT ON NECK

The dumb, uneducated or brainwashed are easily rabble-roused, feeling smart even when soused.

The male bashing is relentless while TV movies show their supposed violence against innocence.

Men are bigger and trained for war so of course it's easy to make them seem like evil monsters.

Everyone takes her side because that's these times and it's all confirmed (continuously) with TV lies.

Men I've known just wanna get along. Peace at any price in fact, they just want tranquility with woman.

One neurotic female pattern is recurrent eruptions out of nowhere. Ladies stay sweet and have flair.

MEN WANT TRANQUILITY, WOMEN SECURITY

Men want tranquility, women want security--but government supports them so why stay skinny?

Looking healthy and fit for her man: that's called fat-shaming now and it's ok to look like a van.

After gender studies they're dumber than when they started--less capable of real world/hardhearted.

Everyone's mad these days: angry, drunk or insane. It's far better to be alone to avoid this drain.

She lost her job due to sexism, not cuz she was late or made messes.

Modern education has replaced intellectual humility with dogma and it's boring, we don't want ya.

Social justice cult graduates and think they have nothing left to learn--all comes down to being burned.

BOOT ON NECK

"Spot the Bigot": That is the focus of every page, sitcom and newscast and we have had it.

Never having a kid's job they aren't happy in the free market and say "I'm oppressed", oh yah.

Western liberal capitalist democracies are where you need to be if you are gay, female, black: free.

The left is more superstition than religion because facts don't matter to them so they never give in.

Love, sacrifice and giving are the highest virtues to Christians but are a laugh to the undisciplined.

They don't care about women they're just being used as tool for central planning and collectivism.

Marketing ploy: Don't you care about women's rights/equality? But it's all collectivism and globalist lies.

FICKLE FEMINISTS

They get along fine then she sees a feminist friend and turns on husband, going way over the line.

For fifty years women have become more miserable as they become more "equal". Why, ingratitude?

A good man is self-sacrificing and generous but now they say feminists have "used all that against us".

In this rabid anti-male environment ridiculous rape claims are heeded no matter how virulent.

Studies show women are 10 X more likely to forgive a terrorist, see him as good or blame his childhood.

Students infected with micro-aggression mentality: attack my politics and it's violence against my identity.

BOOT ON NECK

"Speech is violent, we will not be silent" more BS by the millennial moronic.

I'll never forget the abuses visited upon us by the progressive left.

The Krazy Kollege Kids are ultra-conformists not free thinkers tho' they fancy themselves in those terms.

Thinking man is good they think nothing of coming to your door and inviting all their friends over.

The founders of this country were Calvinists, Puritans and then cowboys and none trusted humans!

Trump is called bigoted, hateful, malevolent. It's just the opposite, he loves America/not out to get us.

TRUMP IS OPPOSITE TO INSULTS

It's true they're brainwashed but still their lower self came out and yuk what a gross draught.

The left envies the raw power Islamic governments have over their people--connection is gov not religion--evil.

Liberals admire how they ruthlessly rule--hating the constitution and human rights they learned in school.

These people are dead, we can't work with them. Trump won, he's our only hope so go inside/ignore dopes.

Dopes don't realize how many of us there are. They'll find out soon, we've got real political power.

Applauding Iran who executes gays and chops off hands. Drug-addicted perverts: the Hollywood scam.

The leftists are complete fascists and will always reject. They're on the dark side but not the elect.

Why don't celebs vacation in Iran? They're like snotty lowlife sophomoric college kids and pro-Islam

BOOT ON NECK

They don't have the intellectual ability to see what they've done funded by Iran.

You put down America for cruelty but Iran hangs gays from cranes.

How is it the left can't see how vacuous they are dangerously aligning with the terror state with the "stars".

Hollywood is heavily homosexual yet loves Iran who kills gays, well?

Hollywood: poor acting, scumbag morals, sell out fakes--silly mistakes.

ZOMBIES CAN'T THINK, EMOTE BY ROTE

Zombies can't think they can only recite by rote

Divide and conquer: Call him "Hispanic" because that's what he is, not "Latino" cuz that is political.

Trump is amazing: the energy, stamina, focus, commitment and delivery is dazzling.

Trump demands fundamental fairness and blocks past hex (TPP) for America every time and for this, thanks.

We won, Trump got in, now don't worry about a thing.

We're sick of political correctness and leftwing totalitarianism. We want common sense of regular folks, amen.

Big gov zealots, ideological fanatics and media promoting PC culture

As Americans feel increased prosperity and security, Trump will trounce the enemy.

As we prosper under Trump, the class/race warfare BS will be harder to sell.

Who dresses in white? Phonies, democrats and the KKK (blights).

The time has come for a new program of national rebuilding. Donald Trump

BOOT ON NECK

They're master spinsters, that's what they do.

It's the style to hate Trump and it's getting old. Public fools, so bold.

They'll eat their words soon, when their finances improve.

So Presidential, so Romanesque, so statesmanly—our guy's the best.

Just shut up. We won and you didn't.

It's only been a few months and he's delivering—blast off, man!

We'll see the end of Hillary and we'll soon see the end of Soros. Alex Jones

Kids fail in school cuz the school failed them.

HORRIBLE RINOS BUT DEMS ARE TRASH

Republicans may be horrible but the democrats are a special type of trash. AJ

A shot in the arm for female entrepreneurs and dems are still disdainful/weird?

Not naming the enemy leads to it's expansion.

Trump's epic and historic speech has split the dems: jump on bandwagon or face liberal abuse and chagrin?

Stole from the taxpayers and gave it to their pals.

Being powerful is like being a lady. If you have to tell people you are, you aren't. Margaret Thatcher

Crybullies on the left were shaken as they watched their globalist dream turn to ash/no more sellout cash.

The time for small thinking is over. Trump will prevail over dem posers.

She thinks it's all her. Even after she copied you she's the star: ignore.

Modern liberal pop Satanism: self-centered people and perversion.

BOOT ON NECK

Trump was an advocate for gay rights for 30 years before it was cool and he loves blacks and women too.

Abortion, a mistake, you're forgiven. But left sees it as a ritual they're lovin'

In a culture in rapid decline the left is openly invoking Satanism: very dark, old and twisted/not Americanism.

Satanism is only powerful against those who don't know what they're facing.

EPA is meant to shut industry down to put it in countries with no controls. To make America defunct, old.

Power grasping pretty boy Paul Ryan is always blocking and lyin'

With each speech Trump's raising up the spirit of America--pride, hurrah

RAISE MORALE, *THEN* RENEWAL

You must raise the morale of a citizenry for them to act properly.

He's got broad shoulders, a big heart but is willing to fight. Mike Pence

See the renewal, feel the renewal: America's coming back again, new.

We must be unified to build a culture and the dems are splitting: closure.

Since man has a fallen nature we're careful who's in power, for sure.

Stock market up 3.9 trillion since Trump

Save yourself ten hours a day, just catch Hannity

Those who the Gods would destroy they would first make mad. Prometheus

A Christian nation with principals astounding in their ability to protect personal freedom.

Violent misogyny is the central point.

There's a reason you don't wanna turn on FOX anymore--go with that.

BOOT ON NECK

It doesn't matter if kids know all 50 states--they just gotta know all 57 genders.

Communism is based on the false dream of utopia so no need for prayer.

Obsession with the environment is a false conscience after God's rejected.

Delete the news, have found time! Update with Hannity, Jones, Savage, Trump.

Russian conspiracy: Neo-Macarthyist paranoia mixed with hysterical self-entitlement/supreme arrogance.

Stop caving to contrived leftist hysteria.

They don't have the moral high ground, but you're on the right side of history while they go down.

It's social engineering on a massive scale. Democrats are the best at this: liberals all tell tall tales.

TRUMP NOT A STATUS CLIMBER

I wasn't elected to spend my time with reporters and celebrities. Donald Trump

Donald J Trump campaigned on speaking directly to Americans and that's exactly what he'll do.

Trump knew about the social tyranny/press-whores and sought to restore power to the individual once more.

Pelosi doesn't know basic facts. She's dumb as a rock and makes no attempt to educate herself, lax.

From trash to treasure in Jesus Christ.

Live inside purpose, path is smooth. Rough path = popular groove.

Liberals are the biggest fascists in the world and that's why they rejected you so forget about it little boy/girl.

They've already committed so many crimes they think they can do whatever they want, but not Trump.

BOOT ON NECK

It's become the Democrat Socialist Islamist Party USA. Michael Savage

When last Christian patriarch died the family swung hard left: totally daft as the social hypnotic depressed.

Survey: 98% of news coverage is anti-Trump.

Reject hex from leftist wrecks.

As the pedophile arrests become massive God's people must fill the void of many openings as the brass leave.

If they don't wanna hear the message, move on. There's too many wounded who need it badly or they'll be gone.

SIN: A MAL-ADAPTIVE COPING DEVICE

Sin is a mal-adaptive coping device (to deal with anxiety) once enticed.

Christian Psychology: Repent of sin, symptoms leave.

Pastors who are not speaking out (e.g. for the unborn) will be silenced and you will see them no more.

I am not ashamed of the gospel of Jesus Christ for it is the power unto salvation. Romans 1:16

Hear Ye: Repent of SIN, symptoms leave. Repent of sin, symptoms leave. Repent of sin, symptoms leave.

The dumb dump on Trump.

The church took a bribe (501c3) and agreed to not talk the truth, so God's judgment will fall soon.

Church took a bribe to not talk about abortion and just look at the evolution.

Johnson Amendment: Pastors shut up when prayer left schools and when abortion became cool.

When the church signed the gag order they signed for judgment.

BOOT ON NECK

The churches wanted tax exempt status so bad they gladly self-censored.

Preaching against sin is "hate speech".

Disinherit the jerks. Jerry Lewis didn't leave a penny to his six liberal sons who never called him Sir.

Millennials think evil is good and good is evil, dark is light and light is dark, bitter' sweet/sweet's bitter.

Our Christian president is removing the Johnson Amendment so pastors can fearlessly speak again.

People won't donate if they can't write it off. So to get donations you get tax status by shutting your mouth.

Pray that God brings total exposure to pedogate and the true motivation of the Trump enemies/hate.

SAME DEAD CORNY SCRIPT

They are following their own corny script and God says "No, sorry--that's been denied" but they continue to lie.

Obama presidency was a complete failure for democrats, he destroyed the dirty rats.

Obama was the tragic culmination of fifty years of liberalism then he did his own party in and I'm lovin it man.

Adapting to liberals was the dregs.
Obama's reappearance is like seeing a bad ex show up--irritation and "why?"

Obama doesn't get people elected he gets them defeated.

Obama did more to destroy the democratic party than the GOP could have hoped or planned: Thanks, man!

The bottom has fallen out of their whole reality. It's called the Ontologically Fatal Insight before insanity.

BOOT ON NECK

Purge is coming: massive pedophile arrests just for a start and this nemesis I'm loving after 8 years suffering.

Haha: the Democrats turn on Obama causing them so much trauma.

Trump gave 25 billion to black colleges, cut 2/3 regulations small business, stocks up 3 trillion: they don't tell us this.

PATRIOTS SAVE US FROM GOVERNMENT

A patriot saves his country from his government. Thomas Paine

This scandal is so massive and all-encompassing I just have to cut out and let the Donald president take care of it.

Facebook banning conservative pro-Trump news. Hello blues

It doesn't matter where they are: People through media are influenced by the same cultural neurosis--bizarre.

Undetectable assassinations like Michael Hastings where cars/planes blow up: that's CIA for decades nonstop.

Turned on FOX--no interest whatsoever. Endless details vary daily but I prefer being constantly clever.

Breaking out of political correctness is the most freeing thing as you find yourself at odds with the whole mess.

Secret Service says Obama had 12 sex hookups a day. This stuff started in sixties: all about sex not "love"--ok?

Feminists maintain the right to kill their babies--this is "gains".

You have no right to bitch having it so good with white man in the west but you support Islam misogynists.

Phony feminists stand for "real family values"--deceivers! You should hear how they talk to husbands in secret.

Phony feminists want open borders--flooded with antithetical cultures. They're dumb as rats, female unthinkers.

BOOT ON NECK

"Better education for girls"--what about boys? We all know how the little boys are squelched, blocked, annoyed.

Discourse over gender became so nonsensical/removed from reality, rowdy resistance is unsurprising. Camille Paglia

They're sycophantic, phlegmatic and pusillanimous: soapy, stodgy and dim.

OLDER WOMEN SHOULD INSTILL MORALS

Older women are to educate the younger on morals. Not an old angry mean female resting on her laurels.

Borrego was filled with angry lesbians. This is not how it is--a blink in history, a deviation.

It's the birds and the bees. It is natural, it is God's will, it is a banquet and celebration, way to be pleased.

This fight ain't over about abortion/homosexuality just cuz you say it is. We say what God says and He's pizzed.

Angry lesbians scared me, they were mean. Borrowing "maleness" is unnatural, a perversion, a new reality unseen.

Men put off by non-nurturing or displeasing females. Demanding, pugnacious self-involved witches, egotistical.

Why does Camille Paglia love "Housewives"? Boring, self-involved, petty, shallow, narcissistic, screaming/snide.

Herd is soapy, phony, stodgy and dim. Give up on em but still be friendly, that's just survival in this lion's den.

Because the opposition is mean we cave in. You have to be bold to go against the false premise which is dumb.

Feminist: Always virtue signaling and act disgusting. Shut up shallow female and stop your sinful lusting.

Concupiscence (tendency towards lust) is in all men and all men are sinners.

BOOT ON NECK

A lousy female housekeeper is shirking her duty. There's a natural division of labor and men bring in the booty.

LIBERAL CHRISTIANS ARE OXYMORONS

It is an oxymoron to be a feminist or liberal Christian.

Both coasts are sick. But they seem to rule what it means to be cool so us bitter clingers are connected and thick.

Designed to take out the small healthcare clinics: a consolidation plan and screwjob by Paul Ryan, a gimmick.

Trump must have his own fireside chats to control the narrative, counter and bypass the blues from fake news.

Taking offense where none is intended.

Who rules determines when they come and get you.

They're putting cancer viruses in vaccines and there's white papers and patents on how they did it.

The cancer viruses go into the nerve and then activate later with stress. They aim to kill 99% of us, what a mess.

Refuse flue shots packed with crap.

Starbucks' leftist stance gains nothing but a bash by the vast majority of conservatives in the world, at last.

How liberals think and begin to stink: Their false premise (anything goes) taken to absurd levels and over the brink.

Both coasts scare me--hotbeds of pomp and vanity.

Guns give you the right comportment: It's an evil world out there, not "good" as we were taught (to ensnare).

Maybe all your life you couldn't let them go, but they're liberals--that's all you need to know.

BOOT ON NECK

Liberals say "it's all good" and other bull. It's an evil world and we gotta be ready, draw lines, bring order, stay still.

Liberals are unprepared cuz it's all about social and that means merged together, unprotected and other bull.

Sorry liberals MLK believed in second amendment rights.

Patriotic red states like Utah are labeled "hostile", trigger gov claws.

We get to elect our president and he is honor bound to accept our will. Obama can't stand it and is here still.

UN-LIBERAL MIDDLE AMERICA

Each time I see the red cliffs of Utah they look different. They are beautiful but best of all: not liberal.

Anarchists are anti-American socialists too uninformed to see how great they have it in the U.S.

True liberalism: hospitality, low taxes, freedom, not judging. Modern liberals: obsessed, neurotic/unloving.

They fancy themselves intellectuals by mimicking silly slogans and sloganizing justifies their shenanigans.

Country folk: the nicest people ever, opposite to the obsessed trendies which are stormy weather.

The schools are actually having fake Trump assassinations and it's all from the liberal teacher's unions.

When nationalism exploded the dems tried to stop the tea party by calling it all "racist" (this was baseless).

Cut taxes, freeze spending and stop endless wars: We're there: total prosperity/innovation galore.

Trump is already presidential and delivering: Not on conquest economies but renaissance for you and me.

At first minorities shunned it but then saw the light on the tea party and now love it: we're in a new orbit!

What they call "fake news" is anything contradicting their leftist narrative: Jones, Drudge, Savage too.

They saw Hillary as more than a president but an idea, a world historical heroine, light itself. Haha

"Hillary is Athena" who can't be faulted, criticized or analyzed--all in the face of behavior we despised.

"Hillary didn't fail us, we failed her": As with all saints and prophets the problem is never them but us.

DISFRIEND LIBERALS TO TEACH THE ABLES

I disfriend liberals to make room for others able/willing to learn.

Hillary was "with out flaws": a peerless leader and benefactor of women and children: Mother Teresa in a pantsuit.

What dummies could make Hillary into a revered pope? Now you know all about your friends the dopes.

The female teachers are totally sexist against the boys. They have no fathers either/likely no toys.

Girls now feel superior to boys at age 4. It's ingrained and if it isn't seen as serious we've no future.

Female teachers give girls better grades than males, but if she doesn't know the sex, females get the fails.

What are his emotional/social skills, ability to get along with the other kids-- assessing non-objective frills.

Bias against boys is perfectly acceptable in society. Teachers smile at girls but frown at boys/it's ugly.

BOOT ON NECK

Black-white achievement gap is large but the gender gap is three times larger/girls seen as smarter.

Now we see why men are checking out: cuz no one cares until the power goes out or we need repairs.

The gender gap in grades goes down one-third when teachers don't know the gender they're marking.

In reaction to sexist rejection boy gets rowdy in class and given an "F" in socialization/end of him.

PUBLIC SCHOOLS ARE TOXIC

Schools are toxic to girls for sure, and boys prejudice and despair.

Men are overly-apologetic about everything cuz they've been socialized that way in the school scene.

Truth: First it's ridiculed then violently opposed then accepted as self-evident: historical pattern, definite.

They hate Donald Trump more than Kim Jong Un and ISIS. It's a riddle and amazing state of psychosis.

More local, more sane--more like you. Here you get your own life back and what a relief: whew.

We've pulled the plug on the swamp now let's make sure it all drains out.

Generation Z is sick of hearing about gender studies, colonialism or the sin of being white, male or whatever.

Liberalism is an echo chamber and a default setting. We've all been tainted by it then wake up suddenly.

Most of the feds aren't bad people but they have special units of democrat scum bags, thoroughly evil.

How did we ever get to this ridiculous point? Creeping: an uninformed public slips into the wrong viewpoint.

Fake news talking heads aren't simply misinformed, they're complicit: taking payoffs, dirty, submissive.

Became part of the enemy through Stockholm Syndrome: an ego collapse then loving the oppression.

The media and education have been weaponized with anti-American rhetoric and it hurts when our kids speak it.

Liberals declare war on cotton and cornbread.

FEMINIST "RAPE CULTURE" BUT ISLAM? UNCONCERNED

First feminists falsify a campus "rape culture" then ignore the real rapists flooding in like vultures.

How to run a household: to cook, clean, raise children well and participate in the neighborhood.

The How To Be a Good Wife skill set has vanished so what's left? Sex, but now it acts as a hex.

When women stopped housekeeping--when those skills were no longer handed down--men were leaving.

Insanity: Wearing a black tent is liberating but a bikini is patriarchy.

Bone and muscle mass, stamina: all different in two genders, hah.

"Transphobic systemic violence" means: advancing the case of fixed binaries (male/female), the crime of "bio essentialism".

"Crime of genocide": describing the male/female divide.

Talk of chromosomes is censured out now by trendies who know.

"Chromosomes determine gender" deleted on Netflix: All of science has gone under, without a fix.

No more "I think therefore I am" but "I'm a victim therefore I am" and I don't exist without it man.

BOOT ON NECK

The insanity of the cultural revolution in 2017. Berkeley is crucial in history of free speech rights/education.

Universities: Free speech only for the left not conservatives, centrists or even centrist liberals.

College administrators are the problem, caving into this and also radical leftist faculty leading this.

Socialism always gives birth to poverty cuz that's the only way you can make sure of everyone's equality.

Socialism gives birth to poverty cuz that's the only way you can make sure of everyone's equality.

HAPPY COMMUNISM IS ILLUSION

Communism is not swaddled infancy forever from hatred and fear of competition cuz it's all illusion.

Attack my politics attack my identity and that's my right to violence: the micro-aggression mentality.

In the Oppression Olympics the white man is at the bottom seen as rotten.

"1 in 5 women raped on campus": LIE. Gang rapes across Europe: ignored by feminists, no outcry.

Trump: Like a light switch prosperity floods back in. Listen up Americans we've never had such a friend.

At anti-Trump demonstrations you can't find anyone who looks normal. These creatures are carnal, awful, immoral.

What they do against Trump fails cuz it's out of grace, not of God and Satanic--thus rappers do it.

They're twisted and bitter against the wholesome: loving families, concern, decency and religion forgotten.

Someone finds the Lord then goes to a church and is shocked by the difference and spiritually blocked.

BOOT ON NECK

Left is so blind, daft and dumb they loved Obama for his big smile alone.

Get that lizard out! Ban him, arrest him, deport him: end our drought.

Everything they say is glowing empty words. That's liberalism: a facade of goodness covering over turds.

Why should we give into stupidity just cuz it yells the loudest and fights in these absurd ways?

By a strange twist of mean fate Pelosi had to face the monsters she herself helped to create.

Haha. Hillary's been supporting Antifa. She's still calling the shots to uproot the deplorables of America.

We thought it was Soros behind it but no it's Hillary who refuses to give up but financing Antifa?

ANTIFA THE ENEMY OF AMERICAN CITIZENS

Real enemy of Atifa: average American citizen.

Defund UC (soon) until they discipline the domestic terrorists called Antifa and rent-a-mob goons.

UC officials are in cahoots with Antifa violence. Defund the campuses or we haven't a chance.

How is Donald Trump a racist? CNN has told Black people he is and otherwise there's no basis.

Pelosi caught in her own web: How do you like confronted by ungrateful brats on the other end?

The most cowardly thing is to fall in with liberal Hollywood and say stupid things about Trump.

The Emmy's are like any trade show--e.g. garbage men giving each other awards. Michael Savage

BOOT ON NECK

Antifa-funder (mean witch) Hillary Clinton: look at their weapons coming against ordinary Americans.

Low-grade idiots like Steven Colbert/failed actor Alec Baldwin are not like patriotic actors back when.

Creeps like Colbert were tearing down family and culture but fortunately their ratings slipped below par.

Not only are primitives seen as more noble, also children being untainted from culture, tho' trouble.

CONFUSED DAYCARE MILLENNIALS

Confused daycare Millennials idiotically fighting for Geo Soro's New World Order yet they don't know.

Emmy's: The talentless low IQ drug addicted puppets caused such a backlash they're out of luck.

It's insane, for Hollywood adoration you should feel ashamed. Specious arguments, I get bored with same.

Jane Fonda hated America then, hates America now--another sick witch seeing herself as highbrow.

As long as your art's about social justice, God's not coming through and the same for any false premise.

A "sexist lying hypocritical egotistical bigot" the stupid witch called Trump the prosperity-spigot.

Feminist say men (and Antifa says whites) are doing things they are not--carelessly they cause riots.

Stop saying men touch "inappropriately"--its the Muslims but you conflate and it's dangerous/silly.

You want to make it look men are bad cuz that's your gig and it's so incendiary saying men are cads.

BOOT ON NECK

They get along fine then she sees a feminist friend and turns on husband, going way over the line.

White men just wanna live their lives and be left alone. Stop blaming--you're not an artist but a clone.

You need a subject so find the closet outlet: leftists are maggots when it comes to that, braggin'

If anything white men are scared of women--the feminists are meaner after talking with their friends.

To make money they turn to trendy topics of scapegoating innocent people/it's really quite evil.

Cuz they hated men they all wanted Hillary who woulda flooded them with misogynists who would kill em.

LIBERALISM VS. WISDOM

There's men and women, dogs and cats, sun and moon. We can see things the liberal way or with wisdom.

You can't dispute these false accusations cuz it's all anecdotal that whites are racist or men claw women.

Instead of using trendy topics why not learn something, take time to mature, you're just a novice.

It's so embarrassing how they virtue signal on trendy topics then expect us to buy it like we're twits.

Dumbed lemmings will believe ridiculous notions of a social hypnotic just cuz the others believe it.

It's not about reason but a bunch of lemmings jumping off a cliff: truth is what the group says it is.

It's a lonely cold atmosphere adapting to liberals cuz it's all about the social and other drivel.

BOOT ON NECK

For my friends everything, for my enemies the law. Oscar Benavides

Homes breaking up over Trump. It comes down to what news do they watch: truth or made up.

The danger they cause: Men are afraid of women who get meaner after talking to the girls (blah-blah).

They brought themselves to their newest, deepest low. Arrogance blinds them but we see/know.

Could've been in the White House ya know, but Hillary's signing copies of her fiction book at Costco.

If the ugly Emmy's don't push you away from liberalism it means you are just too far gone.

AMERICAN TRAGEDY: MILLIONAIRES COMPLAINING

The American tragedy: millionaires speaking on how they are an oppressed minority/need sympathy.

Rappers bash trump to revive their faltering careers but since they stooped so low we kicked em all downstairs.

Stupid Bow Wow and uncle ruined careers forever cuz they went so low.

In obscure loser (washed up rapper) news, Bow Wow is back.

You act cool in a little boy's world saying kidnapping wives for sex slavery is good but it's over for you, hood.

BowWow sass: some day the good Lord will visit you with justice.

Only the dumbest buy liberal lies but fake news the clear despise.

The last refuge of tyrants is war when they're hanging on by their fingernails.

She wasn't social but had the feminist influence: divorce is good, men are bad. She was wrong, he wasn't a cad.

BOOT ON NECK

What is an ugly old bag? An older female who doesn't educate youth on morals but is a dirty thief herself.

He's very "nice" as he ruins his country. ALL liberals with out fail are virtue signalers and it makes money.

Violent threats against the president are now ok?

Everything they do turns to crap and blows up in their face but they don't care--they're moving forward.

You say something wrong and you're removed from society never to be heard from again: family and friends.

The people have not been in charge for so long we've forgotten what it was like and everything's verboten.

RIGHT-WINGERS AND BITTER CLINGERS

I just wanna be with patriots: the right-wingers and bitter clingers.

Tell em "this is immature--virtue signaling to a trendy topic."

Adapting to liberal idiots caused insanity/decades lost, but it's like being in jail: it built character/I'm the best.

No more situational ethics, "going with the flow" or "historical evolution" (legislating the courts by politicians).

Millennials the most servile, brainwashed, evil creatures you can imagine but gen. Z is opposite/can be friends.

He's used to getting things his way ("you're fired"). Worried about his emotions with this/getting too tired.

The Art of the Deal is not working with a crippled, social warrior, obstructive and bought off government.

It's a corrupt evil communist government.

Why aren't filthy dirty rap stars thrown into jail? We want justice, we're sick of it and fear USA is failed.

BOOT ON NECK

Just look at the trashy broken streets of a decaying degenerate municipality ruled by corrupt liberals.

Truth is opposite to appearances, based not on what everyone thinks (herd view) but on facts and sciences.

ALL advancing their own career so true leaders watch out who whispers in their ear, learned from Caesar.

Skilled dealmaker unwilling to strike compromises blew up. How to get other things done? Get rid of Brutus Ryan

Different groups commit different crimes and that's not a racial slur it's cold hard reality/the new paradigm.

Some are 6X more likely to rob, some twice as likely to murder but liberals say "we're all the same", oh brother.

Stats on groups and their crimes don't say why it is, just that it is.

Academics plot against each other, undermine. Backbite, connive to advance over like bureaucrat guys.

FEMINISTS HATE MEN

Stop your blanket accusation of "men". Women had it made with western white men but you conflate again.

Big cities are a threat to the health, the wealth and the liberty of mankind. Thomas Jefferson

Defeat political correctness, secure borders, explode stocks, arrest pedophiles and defund sanctuary cities.

Love of liberty, freedom and ideas unites us--not skin color--but the social engineers don't want that, it's war.

They just wanna feel they're part of a successful group (not be part of real freedom/prosperity) so stay duped.

Progressives are the new Puritans: joyless and authoritarian.

BOOT ON NECK

Justice warrioring degrades your art and holds you back. Stop conforming and be a true artist not a sad sack.

Left thought they had cornered "cool"--can't imagine the right could be the new counter-culture to rule.

Census will now ask gender identity.

You can put a sheep with a lion but only one's coming out in the morning.

Problem with appeasement: you get weaker and the enemy stronger.

Liberalism stinks yet it's been a cultural worldview for decades, making decisions and saying what to think.

UNIVERSITIES FURNISH ILLEGAL TRUANTS

Universities are now stealing all resources from American students and giving them to illegal truants.

Feminists conflate like "all" men rape but are unconcerned for the female victims of the Muslim faith.

The biggest enemy of women is women, and that ignorance is a catastrophe.

Feminist: lies about the wage gap, lies about campus rape culture, stop.

Electricity from Clean Coal costs 25 % of the cost of natural gas and 1/6 of the cost of windmills/solar panels.

So long as crap is filtered through the lens of social justice and identity politics for a start, it's considered "art".

Conceptual art has profound thinking behind it. But the current junk-shop art of ordinary things--forget it.

If people say it's "art" it's "art" even though it's rubbish. These are conformists not dissidents producing trash.

You can't ever please the permanently offended "identitarians".

BOOT ON NECK

Modern art is a physical manifestation born of the demented minds of social justice warriors. Paul Joseph Watson

Feminism: an excuse to treat men like crap. Milo

They think that tingle is giving them power but it's just sucking them down, soured

I see no conflict between being powerful and feminine but liberals do, the fools.

Political correctness promotes pedophilia.

Making a cultural dent is a turkey shoot cuz they're **SO** dumbed down: pursue!

Your enemy splits off then rises up against you and then he gets his whole tribe to do it too.

JAIL RABBLE LIKE BOW-WOW AND UNCLE

Jail BowWow and uncle.

Trump refused to shake the dirty culprit's hand like the other politicians-- that proved who he was, again.

Adverse possession (squatting) succeeds. 120 days to evict and other regulatory obstructions and proceeds.

Manipulators with their own agendas, that's the mainstream news in America.

Trump a horrible racist? How ridiculous!

He knows 15 moves ahead where everyone's going so we get mad at him then later see his game plan.

They undermined him, set him up for a fall, his own advisors that's all.

Truth is alive and lives@Infowars, lies and elitism fight for their lives@Time.

BOOT ON NECK

Justice warrioring degrades your art and hold you back. Stop conforming and be a true artist not a sad sack.

Obama was the reason sun shined and birds sang (while nation can hang) yet Trump over-delivers and it boomerangs.

Tell em "this is immature--virtue signaling on a trendy topic."

So Obama insider "Gibbs" was behind the MacDonald Trash-Trump Tweet. Good sleuthing now it's all complete.

I was so sweet til they got ahold of me. Got no friends cuz they read the papers and idiots won't be seen with me.

The major reaction of the wife of the alcoholic is to get drunk herself, then they blame her more, repelled.

LIBERALS CAN'T ACCEPT DEFEAT

Libs continue to pound that Hillary won, as if our founders ever wanted rule by a mob.

We elected someone to clean it up and he's doing it--looking up!

Fascism came to America under the guise of liberalism: total control/no freedom.

After Hillary Clinton, Maxine Waters and many other feminists people might disdain having women in office.

They don't care about Benghazi, Kidafi, Haiti or Pizzagate (etc. etc. etc.) they just love Hillary.

Virtue signaling/identity politics: a fraud but women suck it up to be mod.

Here's the same old divide, women. Only one solution, don't talk to em.

Unable to see their faults they assume it's prejudice against women. Their own denial blinds them, again.

There is right and wrong. Absolute morality, not relativism of the throng.

BOOT ON NECK

That's not killing it's defending against an aggressor coming against you or it's an unjust war/sinning.

It's so scary how much women love Hillary not caring what she's done whether Kadafi, Haiti or Benghazi.

Hillary could get in if enough dumb women or wimpy feminist men.

Weak leaders have paralysis in fear of retaliation.

If the church doesn't talk of sin they're just social hall religion, a need to be seen and so incredibly boring!

CHURCH OMITS SIN—THE MAIN THING

All wars began with a false flag to gin up support. WWII killed 50 million and the left wants nuclear--come Lord!

A Christian holiday. How wholesome, how sweet, a rare treat, a meaningful revival to ruminate about and tweet.

Truth is the opposite to appearances, based not on what everyone thinks (herd view) but on facts and sciences.

Juan and Geraldo are boring, liberal, aggravating speedbumps yet they're on FOX constantly. Yuk.

Why would Assad wanna kill his own people? He's a crazy man in a country filled with factions, many evil.

Conservative = textualist, by the book.

No analysis of Hillary allowed: Benghazi, emails, Libya were just pseudo-scandals, stuff made up, fowl.

Why they cry? Because their savior, light itself, Athena was extinguished: archetype, demolished.

If they assimilate it's different but if they don't they're "citizens", right? Liberals don't care about our life.

Liberal family members are always offended. That's their whole thing when coming against the splendid.

About Trump: Give him a chance, watch close and wish well. Cheer what's sound, criticize what isn't and tell.

What to tell your scared kids: the left did this, demonizing Mr. Trump and making him monstrous.

The left is irate over it's own false narrative.

After getting news focus on inner peace or die--for "men's hearts will fail them" from fear or media lies.

HIX POLITIX UPDATES 2021

In some states trespassing is no longer a crime. Imagine that--privacy is gone, no more sublime.

In some states shoplifting is not a crime. This is all against the rich--communism is coming.

To appease their open border base progressives are destroying our country with invasion ok?

If you complain of election integrity they put you under investigation not the crooks. Donald Trump

We can't fix immigration with big government socialists in charge cuz they want open borders.

The biggest fruit of hard work is PRIVACY but that's being attacked by the commies see.

Covid 19 is cover for worldwide corporate fascist takeover w/communism as operating system.

Infrastructure means the left's pet projects plus payback for their biggest donor backups.

BOOT ON NECK

Liberals want open borders due to false cosmology, "we are one" and other green age fallacies.

It's terrifying to me. Who's gonna stop this constant flow? It's the end of the country if we don't.

Because Biden and Pelosi take orders from the broadsquad of radical commie socialists they're resisted.

Commies wanna destroy what makes this country great: liberty, freedom, constitution, capitalism.

HOMESTEAD UPDATES

Extraction is King. Get the Bullet: one third frozen fruit/greens/nut butter. Eat & fast 24 hours.

Fruit smoothies, cliff bars, bread/honey, soups/cereal, yogurt dips/mushroom stroganoffs, dates.

I feel phyto-chemicalized after my raw veggie dipped into yogurt green goddess and it's a new trip.

Reducing processed foods while increasing natural rids us of hopelessness, anxiety and depression.

The raw vegetables/high fiber yesterday resulted in extreme gut pain--it's the Fiber Menace again.

At this point it's what can I eat without a bad reaction, not what is good for me but what digests easy.

Retirement is actually what I'd call "time to do what you want" or to be put first, seclude, take naps.

The immature move into a neighborhood and get involved with the neighbors--this is dangerous.

A beautiful country neighborhood becomes a gas chamber when burning trash with plastic sir.

Multiple Chemical Sensitivities--immune deficiency--raises sensitivity so can't stand phones either.

A ringing phone is the biggest abuse. It's pure intrusion, interruption, me having to adapt to THEM.

The less I do the more gets done. Looking out the window with music is most profitable.

Fame brings insults so that's your next obstacle: practice ignoring what the dumb say even uncle.

THE HERD IN WORDS
HIX POLITIX
HOW THEY RUINED US
JUST SKIP DINNER
LE FEMME AND THE COMMUNIST SPIRIT
LIBERAL CHAOS & ROT
LIBERAL DOUBLETHINK
LIBERAL GALL 1 & 2
LIBERAL SHOVE-DOWNS
LOCK YOUR GATE
LOSERS and Femme Fatales
MANUAL FOR SUPERIOR MEN
MODERN ART FROM HELL
MOSTLY FAKE
NOTES TO CHAMPS 1 & 2
OVERCOME FRENEMIES
PC MAKES US CRAZY
PEOPLE ARE CRUEL
PEOPLE PROBLEMS 1 & 2
PERSECUTED GENIUIS
POLI-PSYCH MYSTERIES
PRETENTIOUS SLOBS
QUEEN BEE
RED NEW DEAL
RETURNING TO FIRST NATURE
SEASON OF TREASON
SEPARATE MEANS HOLY
SOCIAL HYPNOTISM
SOLITUDE SOLUTION
SUPERCILIOUS
THE SCHOOLS SCREWED EM UP
TOAD TO PRINCE
TRIALS CYCLES
TRUMP VS. GROUP
TRUST IN TRASH
THE TRUTH ABOUT PEOPLE
UNDERHEANDEDLY CLEVER
WALK TALL WITHIN WALLS
WE'RE NOT ALL ONE
WINNERS SKIP DINNER
WORK OR SMERK

KAREN KELLOCK PH.D.

M.S. Political Science, San Diego State. Ph.D. in Psychology, University of California Irvine. Postdoctoral: UCI School of Medicine, Dept. of Psychiatry [NIMH Grants]. Developed the Debris Theory of Disease, a theory of system pathology in 120 books and 22 textbooks for the general public. The theory has a general formula: All disease is obstruction, all recovery is elimination, all success is attraction. The three obstructions are people, habit and food. Remove obstruction and snap to your goals, waiting in the wings.

www.ingramcontent.com/pod-product-compliance
Lightning Source LLC
Chambersburg PA
CBHW061723250726
48657CB00002B/735